HOPE FOR THE FUTURE
THE NEW EARTH

Neva F. Davis

TEACH Services, Inc.
P U B L I S H I N G
www.TEACHServices.com

World rights reserved. This book or any portion thereof may not be copied or reproduced in any form or manner whatever, except as provided by law, without the written permission of the publisher, except by a reviewer who may quote brief passages in a review.

This book was written to provide truthful information in regard to the subject matter covered. The author assumes full responsibility for the accuracy of all facts and quotations as cited in this book. The opinions expressed in this book are the author's personal views and interpretation of the Bible, Spirit of Prophecy, and/or contemporary authors and do not necessarily reflect those of TEACH Services, Inc.

This book is sold with the understanding that the publisher is not engaged in giving spiritual, legal, medical, or other professional advice. If authoritative advice is needed, the reader should seek the counsel of a competent professional.

Copyright © 2013 TEACH Services, Inc.
ISBN-13: 978-1-57258-888-2 (Paperback)
ISBN-13: 978-1-57258-889-9 (ePub)
ISBN-13: 978-1-57258-890-5 (Kindle / Mobi)
Library of Congress Control Number: 2012916324

All scripture quotations, unless otherwise indicated, are taken from the New King James Version®.
Copyright © 1982 by Thomas Nelson, Inc.
Used by permission. All rights reserved.

Published by
TEACH Services, Inc.
P U B L I S H I N G
www.TEACHServices.com

Introduction

Our story begins after this old earth—with all of the evil people, evil things, and earth's pollution, physical and spiritual—has been burned up and completely destroyed. Then, the Lord will "create new heavens and a new earth" (Isa. 65:17), which will be so fresh, clean, bright, and lovely that it is hard for us to even imagine it! The Bible says, "Eye hath not seen, nor ear heard, neither have entered into the heart of man, the things which God hath prepared for them that love him" (1 Cor. 2:9).

Let us thoughtfully consider and picture in our minds how wonderful our lives will be after the resurrection, when our Lord will give us the gift of a new and perfect body. If that weren't enough, He will also give us a new and most beautiful earth for us to inhabit and enjoy.

The setting of this story is the New Jerusalem after the destruction of the wicked. Imagine all the possibilities of the new earth as you read this story. Envision that you have just arrived in heaven and are learning many new things about it. As

Hope for the Future

I don't know your angel's name, I will simply call him Mark.

Christ's second coming appears to be very near. May we be ready to meet Him when He comes in the clouds to take His children home. Dream with me about what our new life and home will be like after Jesus comes to rescue us from this sinful planet.

Chapter 1

You are sitting alone reading in your home in the New Jerusalem. The front door and windows are open so that you can enjoy the warm breeze. While you are relaxing, you hear a knock on your front door. When you look up, you recognize your special angel who has been so kind, caring, and helpful to you throughout the years. Since arriving in the New Jerusalem, you appreciate the fact that he never seems to tire of answering your many questions.

"Come in, Mark! Come in," you call.

"Not this time," he replies with a smile. "I have some very special news for you! I have been instructed to tell you that the new earth property, which the Lord has prepared and assigned to you, is now ready for you to inspect and take ownership of. Would you like to go and see it now?"

"Wonderful!! Oh yes, let's go," you exclaim as you hurry outside.

You and Mark walk along the golden streets. Soon, you turn onto another translucent gold-paved street, which shines in beauty ahead of you. It is located to the left of the river of life, which flows from the New Jerusalem. The strip of land between the road and the river is like a beautiful park, hence the name Riverside Park Road.

The cool, crystal clear water of the river is pure and drinkable, and it makes a soothing sound as it flows over the precious stones of various colors that line the bottom of the deep riverbed. Here and there you notice gold nuggets flashing brightly in the sun's rays. Mark explains that precious stones and metals are easily available for any of your projects. Lush green grass covers the gentle slope leading down to the river's edge, where some delicately tinted blue and lavender irises thrive. Smoothly polished marble benches nestle among bushes, which are heavy with large and brightly colored flowers. The whole scene is inviting, and you decide to stop for a while to enjoy the soft perfume of the flowers.

Nearby bushes are covered with juicy red berries on which birds of all colors are dining. They flit from branch to branch, pecking at and eating the berries and the seeds from nearby flowers. Occasionally, they burst out with a sweet trilled song.

"What a beautiful picture they make!" you say. "Would those birds allow me to touch them?"

"Why don't you check it out," Mark answers as he sits down on a marble bench. "Just go across the road and pick up a few nuts from under that pecan tree and offer them to the birds and see what happens."

You get the nuts, break them open, and hold them out in your cupped hand toward the birds. In a soft voice, you coax, "Come, little bird. Come to me. Come see. Come see."

A flashy red cardinal perks up and decides to come over and investigate. He lands lightly on your thumb, so lightly that it feels as if no weight at all. He looks up at you, and then his feet tighten on your thumb as his throat swells with his cheerful whistle. He allows you to touch his back; then cocking his head to one side, he checks out the nuts, picking one up and then dropping it, after which he finds one that pleases him. Taking it in his beak, he flies away to a branch with his treasure. You take a deep breath and say, "That was really fun!"

"Yes." Mark answers, "there are a lot of great joys in heaven, but there are many little joys like that which you just experienced. I would say that, especially for people who enjoyed bird watching on the first earth, that they will find pleasure in interacting with the birds in heaven."

As you continue on your way, you admire the trees that line the road, but you especially enjoy the leafy shade of a colonnade of very tall and stately elm trees, which someone has planted along both sides of the road. Their graceful branches are gently moving in a cooling breeze. You take a deep breath of its freshness and exclaim, "Oh, what a beautiful day!"

Mark agrees," Yes, but here on the new earth every day is a perfect day!"

As you walk you see a man approaching from the opposite direction. His easygoing sauntering gait somehow looks familiar. Could that possibly be your old wartime pilot buddy, Gene? He was a self-indulgent, fun-loving sinner who brushed you off when you tried to talk seriously with him, but he is in heaven! You rush toward him, and throwing your arms around him, you cry out, "Gene, I'm so glad to see you! How wonderful that you are here!" You stand back and look him over. "Tell me, Gene, what happened?"

With a slow smile of satisfaction, he answers, "Well, when you thought I wasn't listening, I really was! I decided to turn away from my wasteful way of life, and I prayed to the Lord, 'If You will have a guy like me, I'm all Yours. I want to be a Christian and to do things Your way.' Thank God, He accepted me, and here I am! I'll always be grateful that Jesus died for my sins so that I could be here."

"Amen, amen," Mark murmurs. "What a wonderful and happy ending to your story! I wish that everyone's story could end that way."

"Oh, but that isn't the end of the story," Gene adds. "I persuaded Ray, another friend of ours, to become a Christian, and now he is here also!"

"That is wonderful news," you say. "We must make plans to all get together soon."

Gene points out the hill where his home is located. You tell him that you will get in touch with him as soon as you can, but now you are on your way to see the place that the Lord has prepared for your country home.

As you walk on Mark says that there will be many people in heaven that you never expected to see there. On the other hand, there will be some people who you thought would be there but are missing because their hearts were not right with the Lord.

As you round a bend in the road, on the left is a very beautiful wooded area. Its stately trees are healthy, huge, and very tall. Their towering branches create a canopy of lacy, green leaves. The wood of these trees is very hard. Their large, straight trunks and their great height give a solemn, cathedral-like effect to the woods. Shade loving wildflowers of all types carpet the floor of the woods. Wild animals are resting here after feeding on lush green grass, flowers, and sweet clover in the meadow beyond the woods.

Hope for the Future

A sleek, sinewy, and beautifully striped tiger notices your passing. He leaves the pack and silently pads behind you. Mark explains that the tiger really wants some attention, so he stops and pats the tiger's head and smooths the sleek fur down his back. The tiger purrs contentedly and arches his back under Marks hand. Then the tiger lopes back to his pack.

As you travel on, you meet more people who are coming onto Riverside Park Road from some side roads. They all greet you with "Good morning!" and a warm smile. It gives you a happy feeling of brotherhood with all of these people, God's precious children, who came from every nation of the old earth. You stop and visit a while with many of the passers-by.

But now, the sound of a soft sweet melody greets your ears from beyond a curve in the road. A few more steps and you see a very pretty, young black mother sitting on a marble bench by the river. She is gently rocking a reed basket that contains a kicking and cooing baby boy. You pause to listen to her sweet lullaby.

Sleep, my baby. Sleep, my dear one.
You are precious, my dear son.
Sleep, my baby. Sleep, my dear one.
Time to rest from play and fun.
Jesus loves the little children,
And He blessed you every one.
Sleep, my baby. Sleep, my dear one.
You are precious, my dear son.

The song fades away. The kicking in the basket ceases, and richly fringed eyelids flutter and close over sleepy dark eyes. All is silent except for the lapping of the water on the river's edge and the soft humming of bees gathering nectar from nearby flowers. The mother is unaware of your presence.

A soft glow of peace and contentment lights her face. She is gazing across the river at some wooly white lambs that are jumping and frolicking on the grassy slopes of the other side of the river. You decide not to break her reverie, but you hope to later make the acquaintance of this sweet singer. A pair of twins, a little boy and girl, complete her family. They have been playing quietly by the side of the road with a small black puppy that sports a white bib and feet.

Since the children are near the road, you stop and introduce yourself and ask them their names. The little girl answers, "My name is Patty, and my brother is Peter. Our little brother in the basket is Perry."

"Those are nice names. Do you love your little puppy?"

"Oh yes! Isn't he cute?" Patty says as she holds him up for your inspection. "Our angel gave him to us yesterday. We promised to take good care of him. We decided to name him Boots because of his white feet."

By this time the puppy squirmed and wriggled his little body out of her grasp and jumped down and raced away for a game of tag. Yet you are faster than the puppy's little legs. You scoop him up as he streaks by and restore him to Patty's arms. She looks up and thanks you with a shy little smile. You pat them both on their heads and say, "Enjoy your puppy. We have to go now. Goodbye!" You wave to their mother who has, by this time, noticed your and Mark's presence and the puppy's escapade.

As you continue on your way, you ask Mark, "Do you know about that young lady's history?"

"Well, I didn't," he answers, "but an angel friend of mine told me about her. Her name is Lucy. She lived in Africa. As a child she attended a Christian school for a short time and learned about the true God of creation. She decided to worship Him and not the idols that were in her home. This made her parents very angry, and she was forced to marry an older man when she was merely a child. He already had other wives and cruelly beat them when he got drunk. Lucy was the only Christian in the family. When the twins were born, she worked extra hard to get food for them, and she tried to help the others in the family as much as she could. At the time when her baby boy was born, their home was located in the worst possible place, right in the middle of two warring tribes. Her husband decided to go and fight, and he left them alone. There was no place to flee to and no place to hide from the enemy. They were all killed. Lucy, Patty, Peter, and Perry were buried. An angel marked their graves and they slept until Jesus came back to earth in great power and glory and raised them back to life along with all those who loved Him but had died. They, along with those who were alive at His return, all received the miracle of a new and perfect body.

"Isn't it nice that people can recognize their friends and relatives here in heaven? You know that the Bible promised, 'We shall know as we are known.' Jesus has given each one a gift of a dazzling white robe and an individually designed precious crown. Even the little children have received a small gold circle for their heads. Everyone also received a portable golden harp and the ability to play it for their enjoyment. As you well know, everyone also received a unique gift of a sparkling white stone with their new name written on it, which no one else knew. It was just for Jesus and them. Were you happy with what was written on your stone?" Mark asks.

"Oh yes, the Lord surely knew very well what I went through."

Mark continues, "He also gave Lucy a beautiful home and a peaceful and happy life here on the new earth. Did you notice how happy and contented Lucy looked?"

"She did seem to have a glow on her face," you agree.

"The nice thing about it all is that what she is now is really only the beginning of what she can be and what she will be able to do in the future. She can develop her talents and interests by attending and learning at the angel classes. I expect her to soon be singing with the angel choir and to be learning the much more intricate and exquisite details of how to compose heavenly music, the harmony of which far surpasses anything ever heard or produced on the first earth."

"I'd like to be able to do that too," you say.

"You may. Actually there is no limit to how much people can learn, grow, and develop intellectually here on the heavenly new earth."

You hear joyous laughter ahead and soon meet a group of children jumping rope in the middle of the street, and no one seems to mind. Of course, there are no cars in heaven! On the park side is a little gem of a garden where neighborhood parents are working, visiting, and keeping an eye on the children at play. The edges of the garden are defined by a neatly trimmed evergreen hedge. A cobblestone pathway leads between flowerbeds of bright spring flowers. Red tulips, cream-colored daffodils, and purple and pink hyacinths add fresh beauty to the scene, and their sweet perfume greets you from along the pathway.

A man named Barry who lives nearby is a talented woodworker. His original home was in Switzerland. He has made attractive and comfortable seats and has placed them at the edges of the garden where people may sit and rest and visit.

Up the road a short distance beyond the garden, you see where the road ascends to a raised bridge, which goes over a rushing mountain stream. Its wrought iron posts and railings are decorated with gracefully climbing gold vines, gold leaves, and flowers of varied colors made of precious stones. They all glow and sparkle in the sunlight. You stand fascinated and amazed by the sight.

Noticing your reaction, Mark says, "Beautiful, isn't it? A man named Timothy is getting quite accomplished in his chosen craft of working with precious metals and stones. In his spare time, he has been working on a number of bridges in the area. If you wish, when the time comes, I'm sure he would be willing to help you decorate your new home. But now, I would like to direct your attention to your left. Please tell me, what do you see?"

"I see," you answer, wondering why Mark is asking the question. "I see verdant and peaceful hills and valleys covered with lush green grass and a scattering of different kinds of trees. I see sheep grazing on one of the hills, and there are lazy white clouds drifting overhead under a warm noontime sun. I also see a mountain stream working its way around the hills and through the valleys until it finally flows under this bridge."

"Yes, yes," Mark gently prods you on. "But what do you see beyond all that?"

"Oh, I see a truly spectacular view of a red mountain. It is mostly covered with emerald green growth, but there is a high red rock cliff where the stream emerges and is soon transformed into a spectacular, sparkling waterfall that cascades, plunges, and splashes deep down into the valley below. As the mist arises, I see a complete rainbow arch that glows with soft blending colors. It looks as if a pathway winds its way back and forth up to some plateaus along the way."

"What do you think about that view?" Mark asks.

"It depicts the most special natural beauty I have seen so far," you answer.

"Good," Mark says as he makes a sweeping gesture with his arm across the scene. "Everything you have described is now your very own, to do with as you please, a gift to you from Jesus."

"How can that be? I am so unworthy!" you exclaim.

"Do you remember that Jesus said in the Bible that if you were faithful over a few things He would make you ruler over many things? Just think, your mountain is big enough that, if you wish, and if they wish, some of your relatives may build on your mountain also, and you and your family could be close together. You did your best to be faithful on the old earth, trying to encourage and help others, even through troubled times.

It gives the Lord great pleasure to do nice things for all of His children," he explains.

"I am overwhelmed. I will always be grateful," you answer.

Chapter 2

You are still trying to take in all that Mark has just told you. The Lord has given you so much, and you stand in amazement at the beauty and immensity of God's wonderful gift to you. As you stand there, you hear the *clip clop*, *clip clop* of a horse's hooves on the pavement beyond the bridge. Soon a large white horse appears coming across the bridge toward you. He is carrying a handsome young rider who is very tall, broad shouldered, and muscular-looking. His face is clean-shaven, and it has a healthy glow. His blue eyes gleam with a sharp intellect, and yet his face bears a kindly and thoughtful expression. He has shoulder-length, wavy brown hair, and he is clothed in comfortable, homespun linen pants and shirt. Reining in his horse close beside you, he jumps down, greets Mark, and holds out his hand toward you.

"Welcome to our neighborhood! My name is Samuelle, but you may call me Sam if you would like. I'm your neighbor. I live on that hill just beyond your property. I was told that you were coming, and I want you to know that I am here to show you around and to help you get settled as much as I can."

Opening the saddlebag, he draws out a basket and hands it to you. "My wife, Nan, thought that you might be hungry, so she sent some lunch."

You pull up a brightly multi-colored linen cloth from the basket, and the enticing odor of freshly baked bread greets your nostrils. "Oh, thank you. That really does make me hungry."

"Well, if it is all right with you," he says taking the basket back, "I'll carry it for you, and we will stop as soon as we find a nice picnic spot on your mountain."

Mark has been standing on the sidelines smiling approvingly. "Well now, since you are in the hands of a very good and capable man, I should be hurrying back to the city as there are things that I really need to be doing there. Oh, by the way, I have prepared a little surprise for you on your mountain. Enjoy," he says with a parting smile.

"Mark, I want you to know that I appreciate everything you have done for me. Thank you, and please tell Jesus that I really love this place even before I've been able to go up on my mountain. It couldn't be nicer! Thank Him for me until I can thank Him in person."

"I will," he assures you. With that he spreads his wings and flies away.

Hope for the Future

You watch him disappear from sight and then you remark to Sam, "Mark has surely been a wonderful friend to me."

"Oh yes, everyone loves Mark," Sam agrees.

Sam turns and smooths his horse's mane and gives him a pat. "His name is Star," he tells you.

"Star is such a beautiful horse," you comment.

"I have more like him in my pasture," Sam assures you. "I would be very happy to give one to you, if you wish."

"I appreciate that. That would be very nice."

"Would you like to take a horseback ride on Star around the foothills and up to the edge of your mountain now?" he asks.

"Oh, yes," you answer. "Thank you." With that, Sam easily picks you up and places you on Star's back and then he climbs up also.

Star is very anxious to get going, and the big horse starts racing up the pathway by the mountain stream. You hold tightly to Sam's back as Star gallops along, but he slows up when several deer and a fawn emerge from a thicket. They gaze at you curiously, but unafraid they start cropping the lush grass by the water's edge. As Star slows down and canters along, you enjoy the warm sun on your back and the cheerful singing of the birds in the trees along the edge of the stream. "Sam, can you identify all those different birds?"

He laughs, "Oh no, but I'm working on it!"

At this time you are coming to the hill where you saw the sheep grazing, and you now see a lion lying in the grass with the sheep! You recall the text from the Bible that depicted this very scene, and you revel in the perfect harmony of heaven, even among the animals.

Now Star comes to a complete stop to allow a mother duck and her fluffy little ducklings to pass over your pathway. Their little legs work hard to stay close behind their mother. She is intent on getting her babies to a small lake on the other side of the pathway.

As you ride on, you begin to hear the faint sound of the waterfall. Soon it grows louder and louder and then the falls comes into full view with a pounding roar!

"Oh look, isn't that beautiful?" you exclaim.

Sam pulls up to a flat, grassy spot, which has a large smooth rock in the middle. "How nice," he says, "here's a perfect table for our lunch and a great view besides."

"I'll second that idea," you say. "I'm really hungry now."

Sam helps you dismount. Then getting the basket down, he spreads Nan's bright-colored cloth over the rock, and unpacks the basket. First he breaks off a big piece of Nan's delicious bread for you, then he hands you the biggest and most beautiful peach you have ever seen and a long green fruit, which has gold and silver stripes. Next comes some light-colored nuts that are new to you. Some little date fruitcakes for desert come after that, and last of all, Sam hands an earthenware cup to you so that you can get a drink from the mountain stream. Sam says the blessing, thanking the heavenly Father for the food.

You take a bite out of the peach. It is the tastiest peach you have ever eaten. Its juicy sweetness is especially delicious, and you savor every bite. The striped fruit has a tart flavor. All the rest of the food is very good. You are curious about the striped fruit and ask Sam about it. "Sam, what is this striped fruit?"

"Well, that is a very special fruit from the tree of life. The tree of life produces a different fruit each month. And people can come every month to pick the new variety of fruit.

"Perhaps you have been wondering why you are shorter and smaller than I am. You see, I am from the descendants of Seth, the son of Adam and Eve. Seth's appearance was very much like Adam, who had eaten from the tree of life, and we all inherited long life, strength, and many talents from them. No written language was needed then. People lived for hundreds of years and passed down stories from generation to generation. The people who had decided to serve the true God of creation were called the sons of God, and we were among that group.

"However, there was another group who were the descendants of Cain, who killed his brother Abel. Cain and Abel were Eve's first children. When Cain was born, Eve marveled at the wonderful miracle of birth. 'I have gotten a man from the Lord' she said. How little did she realize how much heartache Cain would cause her later on in his youth by making her lose both of her firstborn children! In a fit of jealousy and anger over the fact that God had accepted Abel's proper sacrifice of a lamb as God had instructed them to do, and not the sacrifice of his own choosing, Cain hardened his heart and killed his innocent younger brother, Abel. After that he turned his back on God and traveled east of Eden to the land of Nod, where he established a city, which he named after his son Enoch.

"You will notice that Cain's people chose names similar to names chosen by the sons of

God. They also inherited the same talents, beauty, strength, and long lives as the sons of God. However, they used these great talents and nature's bountiful supply of gold, silver, and precious stones to glorify themselves and their homes. They tried to outdo their neighbors, and they finally got to the place where they would steal and kill just to get what they wanted. They sought to forget the God of creation entirely."

Sam pauses, but you urge him to continue. "Please tell me more. I am fascinated by how life was in that time of the earth's early history."

"I will," he answers, "but first we must start climbing up your mountain." He gathers up the rest of the lunch, folds the cloth, and places it in the basket. Then he turns to his horse and says, "Star, you stay here until we come back."

As you walk up the mountain path, Sam resumes his story. "I had two younger brothers, Jude and Jared, who had musical talents. They decided to teach music and to make a business of dealing in musical instruments. They had heard that the very best of instruments were being crafted at the town of Enoch. They wanted to check them out and to buy some instruments if they were as good as reported. If their business grew, they could buy more. Nan and I didn't get involved in my brothers' music venture as we already had a pottery business.

"My father wasn't happy about my brothers having anything to do with Cain's tribe, but they argued that they had the best instruments available and that they would do their business and wouldn't terry. They promised to come straight home when they had finished.

"Jude and Jared traveled to Enoch and went straight to the city center to inquire as to where they could find the man who manufactured the musical instruments. Seated on the edge of the city well were two of the most stunningly beautiful young ladies my brothers had ever seen! It was obvious that they came from a wealthy family by the way that they were dressed. The shorter girl, a curly-haired blond wore a very softly draped robe of pink, which was belted by a filigreed gold belt studded with turquoise gems. Her dangling turquoise earrings reflected her beautiful blue eyes. A narrow gold band held her curls in place. Gold ankle bracelets with tiny bells made a tinkling sound as she moved.

"Her older sister, a taller, dark-haired girl, was very sophisticated. Her long, heavy black hair was braided with gold cords and coiled on the top of her head. Her emerald green gown was caught up over one shoulder and fastened with a rosette of emerald jewels that matched her green eyes. Jude walked over to them and introduced himself. 'I am Jude from the sons of God tribe, and this is my brother, Jared. We are musicians and have traveled here to find the famous man who crafts those super musical instruments we've heard about.'

"The girls laughed, and the older sister introduced herself, 'I am Suzann, and this is my younger sister, Barbette. The reason we were laughing is that "the famous man" who you want to see is our dad, and we would be happy to take you to his shop.' With that they jumped up and started toward their home. They explained that their father had several wives and that they were half-sisters. Workmen had been replacing some of the stones in the plaza, and Jared almost stumbled into one of the holes, but Barbette reached out and pulled him toward her, thus preventing a bad fall. An unfamiliar and strange thrill swept over Jared at the touch of her jeweled hand. He was embarrassed but quickly recovered and thanked her. They walked on. Soon they arrived at the girls' home, which was an imposing large mansion with a gated yard. Their father's business was located right next to their home.

"The girls took my brothers inside the shop, introduced them, and then left. It was a large room with benches along one side where craftsmen were working and long triple shelves on the other side of the room displayed the instruments. Special woods had been used, and they were carved and shined to perfection. Jude played a short song on the harp, and they tried out several of the other instruments. The quality of the sound of each one was excellent. They were very impressed, and they bought as many as they could carry. Suzann and Barbette were waiting by the gate, and they waved and called out to my brothers, 'Come back soon!'

"The boys waved back and then walked along quietly until they got outside of the city. Jude finally commented, 'Know what? I think those girls like us!' And they did, as we found out later. They had said to their mothers, 'Those young men from the sons of God are so polite and kind, not at all like the young men that we know around here who are rough and self-centered.'

"On the way home Jared said, 'That little blond, Barbette, is so attractive. She just bubbles! She's the one I like best.' Jude retorted, 'That's a good thing that you feel that way because Suzann is more sophisticated. She has a quiet dignity that I like. I would choose that kind of beauty any day!'

"When Jude and Jared arrived home, the beautiful girls were all they could talk about, but to us only, not to our father. Of course, he soon found out what had happened, and taking them aside, he warned them, 'Boys, you don't realize the danger you are in! You must put a stop to these relationships before they go any farther.

The joining of God's people and Cain's people can only lead to unhappiness and perhaps the loss of eternal life in the end. Please look among our group for some nice, God-fearing young women.'

"As time went on, my brothers' business prospered, and they needed to go to Enoch to purchase more instruments. This time they were better prepared, and they took horses to carry a big load. They went straight to Jubal's shop, and he greeted them warmly saying, 'Welcome back! Did you come to purchase more instruments? We have produced several new instruments to add to our collection since you were last here. I think you will like the sound of this one.' Then he showed them a new flute-like instrument that had a very sweet tone. Jared quickly caught on to the way it should be played.

"Then Jubal said, 'Oh, I almost forgot! I know a couple of young ladies who would be very upset if I didn't let then know that you are here.' Then he asked one of his workmen to go get Barbette and Suzann. When he found them, they actually came running in toward my brothers. Jared said that Barbette looked so charming and cute trying to hold up her long skirts and run that he gave her a little hug when she got to him, to the applause of the workers who had been watching. Suzann took Jude's hand in both of hers, and they walked off together since the girls wanted my brothers to meet their mothers. Their mothers gave them lunch, and they had a nice visit, after which they said their goodbyes. This time they left after giving the girls big hugs and promising to come back again soon. They went back to the shop, picked out the instruments they wanted, learned how to play the new ones, and then loaded up their horses and went home.

"My brothers started building nice homes for the girls. They had fallen in love and were determined to have these beautiful girls for their wives. The girls promised to serve their husbands' God when they were married. After all, there were many household gods in their father's home, and they could easily change to a different one! After the weddings, they actually did attend the solemn weekly Sabbath services where the sons of God all went to the gates of the Garden of Eden to pray and to offer the lamb as a sacrifice. The sacrifice was to remind them that the Son of God would offer Himself as a sacrifice for their sins so that they could have eternal life.

"After Barbette became pregnant, she protested that she couldn't travel and go to the Sabbath services in her condition; however, she never went to the Garden of Eden after that. A sturdy, little blond boy was born to them, and he was the pride and joy of Jared's life. They named him Troy. Troy was very bright and a quick learner.

He was still very young when Jared taught him to play the flute.

"About this time Barbette decided that it was time for her to take Troy and go back to Enoch to visit her family for a few weeks and to have her mother's dressmaker replenish her wardrobe. When she came back home, she showed Jared a very beautiful and expensive gift that her mother had given her. It was a gold-covered statue of a woman who had long flowing hair. She was wearing a long gown and a crown on her head. Her hands were outstretched. Barbette said it was to decorate their garden, and she placed it in the middle of a round flowerbed that was surrounded by flat stones going around it and to it.

"One afternoon when Jared came home from work to get something, he heard music in the garden, and he went out to listen. What he saw was very upsetting to him. Little Troy was playing his flute as he did a simple dance step while making his way around and around the flowerbed. Every time he arrived in front of the gold statue, he picked a flower and placed it in the outstretched hands of the statue. Barbette did not see Jared come as her back was toward him.

"'Barb, what are you doing?' he burst out with emotion. 'Troy, run over to the shop and ask Uncle Jude if he has time to teach you a new tune.' Troy skipped away and then Jared said to

Barbette, 'You know I don't want idol worship in our home!'

"Barbette ran to Jared and threw her arms around him and said soothingly, 'Oh my dear, I love you and our little Troy so much! I was only teaching him a simple dance step that my own mother taught me when I was his age. I do wish that you weren't so tight laced and narrow minded!'

"He answered her, 'The true God in heaven, who created us and cares for us, is the only One who we should worship and not senseless idols.' He then walked away. But the seed had been planted for change, and gradually, imperceptibly, bit by bit, it happened almost without his realizing it. He loved his family, and he wanted a peaceful home, so he often gave in to her wishes just to avoid an argument.

"Things were not always easy for Jude and Suzann either. At first she was lonesome for the pressured and busy city life of Enoch. Jude treated her with love and kindness but was firm in his determination to serve the true God who had blessed them so much. She gradually grew to like the easy going and peaceful rural life of their sons of God, and she decided that she would serve their God also.

"Two years after Troy was born, Jude and Suzann's little girl was born. She inherited

Suzann's dark-haired beauty and Jude's talent for music. Yet best of all, she had a very sweet and loving disposition. They decided to name her Melody as she bought such joy to their home. Jude composed a song called 'Sweet Melody,' which he sang to his baby girl, and she would laugh and wave her arms to the music. She could already sing simple songs when she was just three years old. When she was old enough, Jude got a pony for her and made a little cart for it to pull.

"Troy and Melody were the best of friends. He had a sort of protective attitude toward her since he was two years older than she was. They enjoyed taking the pony cart down to the river to search for gold nuggets and pretty stones, which they piled into the cart and brought back home. Occasionally they were allowed to take the pony cart the short distance to Grandpa Adam and Grandmother Eve's home, which they loved to visit. Troy would jump out of the cart and run ahead to try to beat Melody and the pony on the way. When they arrived, Grandpa Adam would carve little animal toys for them, and he would tell them about the joys of the Garden of Eden. He would explain how kind God had been to them even though they had sinned by eating the fruit they had been forbidden to eat and that God had made a plan by which Jesus, His Son, would come to earth and bear their punishment so that they and anyone else who wished could obtain eternal life by accepting His offer.

"Grandma Eve was perhaps the most beautiful woman who ever lived because she was God's perfect gift to Adam to be his friend, his companion, his helper, and his dear wife, whom he loved very much. Eve told them how happy she had been at the birth of her children. She considered them a miracle, a wonderful gift from God. She would give Troy and Melody hugs and a lot of treats to take home with them when it came time to go.

"As they grew older, Troy and Melody attended classes at their fathers' shop. Melody loved to sing, and she learned to be a very good little singer. Troy enjoyed his classes, and it wasn't long before he could play all of the instruments they had in the store.

"After some time, when Troy was ten years old, Jared invited the whole family over to his home, as he had an important announcement to make. He said, 'My father-in-law, Jubal, has made an extremely generous offer to us. If we will move to Enoch, he will make me a partner in his very profitable business, and he will build a beautiful mansion for us right next to theirs. This will make Barbette's mother very happy.' I saw a shadow of doubt and sadness quickly pass over his face, but he went on resolutely, 'We have decided to accept this generous offer. Don't feel sad that we are leaving. We will be seeing you.' He sold his house and gave most of the money to Jude. We helped him load the few things that they were taking with them onto a wagon. We said our sad goodbyes, and Melody started to cry as we watched the wagon and our dear ones travel over a hill and disappear from sight.

"We heard that Jared entered into life in Enoch with gusto. He was an asset to Jubal's business, and he quickly took charge of planning the town's festivals and feasts. There was always some entertainment going on. Except for business trips, we didn't see him often. After about five years, we received an invitation to an imposing second wedding from Jared as he was taking one of Barbette's younger sisters for his second wife, but we didn't go to the wedding.

"There were some very dedicated people like Enoch and Methuselah who would occasionally travel into Cain's territory and try to persuade some of the people to come back with them and worship the true God of creation. Not many came; however, our people persisted, and a few did come, but even of those who came not all of them stayed. Some wanted to go back to their exciting and sinful ways.

"Some years later, one of my relatives, a cousin named Dan, decided to travel to the city of

Enoch to preach to the people. It was one of their many holidays, and a crowd of people were milling around at the city square. Some were already drunk! He climbed up on a bench, raised his voice so that all could hear, and earnestly tried to persuade them to leave their idol worship and frivolous and sinful ways, which could only lead to an unhappy end. He invited them, 'Come back with me to the land of the sons of God where we worship the true God of creation, who has promised eternal life to those who serve Him, because of the sacrifice which the dear Son of God, Jesus, will make to atone for our sins.'

"Dan noticed a tall, blond, and very handsome young man on the fringes of the crowd pressing forward to better hear his words. When the crowd dissipated, the young man introduced himself, 'My name is Troy, the son of Jared. I do believe that you are right in what you say about worshiping the God of creation, and I would like to come back with you to the land of the sons of God. I spent some happy childhood days there, and I would like to serve the true God of creation again.'

"Dan embraced him and told him, 'You are my relative, and we would be very happy to have you come and live with us until you can make your own plans.'

"'Good,' Troy replied, 'but first I must go and

say goodbye to my parents. I need to gather up a few belongings, and I'll also need to get some money for expenses.' He had some savings. When they arrived at Jubal's shop, they noticed a beautiful horse tied by the road in front of the shop.

"'That is Beauty, my father's favorite horse. He is training him to be a race horse,' Troy explained as Dan tied his horse next to Beauty. They found Jared doing inventory.

"'Father,' Troy said quietly, 'there is something I need to tell you.'

"'What is it, my son?'

"'This man is a cousin of ours. His name is Dan, and he was talking in the city square about coming back with him to the sons of God tribe and joining them in the worship of the true God of creation. I have decided that this is something I should do.'

"A fleeting look of amazement, shock, and consternation passed over Jared's face, but after a short pause he answered, as he placed his hand on Troy's shoulder, 'Troy, I love you very much, and I surely do hate to see you leave, but I know, in my heart, that you are doing the right thing. I never would try to stop you, so go with my blessing.'

"He continued, 'I know that there isn't a lot of money over there, so allow me to give something to you to help you to get started.' He gave Troy a leather bag containing a large amount of money. Troy thanked him, and they embraced and said goodbye.

"As Troy started down the path where the horses were tied, Jared came to the door and called, 'Troy, take Beauty. You will need him.'

"Troy rushed back to his father and exclaimed, 'Oh no, Father. Beauty is your very best and favorite horse. I don't want to take him.'

"'I insist,' Jared said decisively as he untied Beauty and handed the reins to Troy. After one last hug, Troy and Dan galloped off, and Jared was left all alone. 'Ah,' he mused, as he quickly brushed away a lone, unbidden tear that streaked down his cheek, 'my actions have come full circle. I left the sons of God to keep the love and companionship of Barbette and Troy and now I am losing both!' He then sadly went back to his work.

"Barbette was very busy overseeing her mansion and the building of another one. Caring for their large family of wives and children and overseeing her household servants was a full-time job. It took a lot of time and effort. When Troy came to say goodbye to his mother, she didn't have too much to say. 'Troy, you're a man now, and you have to make up your own mind.' So with a hug and a goodbye they were on their way.

At this point of the story, Sam added his own experience. "Shortly after Troy came back to us,

Hope for the Future

I took a trip to Enoch to see Jared as I wished to persuade him to come back with me. He told me how sad it made him feel to see Troy leave, but he just couldn't leave. After all, he was so very involved. He said that he had a big family there. He was a respected member of the city council and had just been elected judge of Enoch and the surrounding land of Nod, and he had acquired a great deal of wealth in Enoch, which he wouldn't be able to do in the stricter society of our tribe, but he added thoughtfully, 'Perhaps later, at a more convenient time, maybe I could come beck.'

"I sadly gave up as I was thinking, 'That more convenient time will never come!' Then I went back home."

Chapter 3

You've been so engrossed by Sam's story that you haven't been paying attention to your surroundings. Suddenly Sam stops his story and says, "Look, we're coming to the first plateau where your special surprise is waiting!" You come back to reality and look around you. In front of you lies a green grassy floor with beautiful shade and olive trees along the edges. Their leafy branches arch over a flat stone pathway in the middle, which leads to an arbor of wooden trellises at the other end of the plateau. The trellises are loaded down with a bountiful display of all kinds of grapes. Some are as big as walnuts! You run down the pathway and start tasting each kind, but your conclusion is that you can't decide which is best.

"When we come back down here, you must take a supply of these grapes home with you."

"No, Mark gave some of these special plants to me when he planted this garden, so I have another grape arbor just like this one on my property."

You sit down to eat a few more grapes and

rest awhile, and after a short time, you urge Sam to tell you the rest of his story about Troy.

"Well, when Dan and Troy arrived at our settlement, Troy left Beauty at Dan's place and walked over to Jude's music store and school to see if his uncle would have a place for him to work. The place had been improved and enlarged since he had last seen it. He walked down a hall that had small rooms on either side for individual classes. It was late in the afternoon, and most of the teachers and students had gone home, but the door was ajar at one room where he heard a sweet soprano voice singing a lilting song that ended on a soft high note. It was as true, clear, and sweet as a bird's song. The voice said, 'There, Molly, that's the way to sing it. You must be careful about flatting that song. Now it is time for you to go home."

"Molly gathered her things, said goodbye, and left. Troy recognized that the teacher was Melody, but she had her back to the door, so she didn't see him. When she turned around, she looked at him in disbelief, for now he wasn't that young boy, her childhood friend, but he was a very tall and handsome young man. 'Troy, is that you?' She ran to him and, putting her arms around his waist, gave him a big hug, and put her head on his chest. 'Troy, I cried when you had to leave,' she said.

"Troy felt a stirring in his heart that wasn't childhood friendship anymore, but he realized that it was far too soon for that sort of thing. He needed to establish a business, and he didn't want to rush her into a closer relationship too soon, as they had hundreds of years ahead of them to make important decisions and plans, so he just patted her on the back and answered, 'There, there, my little friend, that young boy shed a few tears also, but he wouldn't admit it. That wouldn't be manly!'

"She laughed. 'Well then, you've come a long way!' she said. 'Have you come to stay, or are you just visiting?'

"'I've come to stay,' he assured her.

"'Do come home with me for supper,' she urged. 'My parents will be so glad to see you, and I'm sure that Dad will have a job for you, if you wish.'

"'Oh no, I'm too travel worn and dirty to come,' he insisted.

"'Travel worn and dirty, who cares? Come on!' she urged again, so he went. 'First, I want to show you my horse Princess,' she explained as they walked. Before reaching the house, they stopped at the stable, and she brought Princess out, a well-groomed, beautiful, and gentle white horse. "Dad gave her to me when I outgrew the pony."

"'What a beautiful horse! I think Princess is just right for you,' he said as she led Princess back

Hope for the Future

into the stable, and they went on to the house.

"Jude and Suzann were surprised and delighted when Melody came in and announced, 'Mom and Dad, look who I brought home with me from school. It's Troy! He just arrived here from Enoch with Dan, and best of all, he plans on staying here with us.'

"They welcomed him and invited him to stay and eat supper with them. After supper they talked about what kind of work Troy could do to make a living. Jude said that Troy could have a job teaching music or he could work as a salesman, but when he found out that Troy had learned the craft of manufacturing musical instruments from his grandfather, Jubal, they decided that they would start a new branch of manufacturing musical instruments in the music company with Troy overseeing the process. Troy offered to put some money into the project to get it started. They needed to find some good craftsmen and train them before they could even start making any money on that part of the business.

"Suzann waited patiently for them to finish talking business, and then she said, 'Troy, did you find it difficult to leave your home and your parents and to come here?'

"'Yes,' he said, 'but I knew it was the right thing to do.'

"'You did the right thing. We will do our best

to be second parents for you here,' she said. 'Your mother and I were very close when we were young. Tell me, how is Barbette doing?'

"He answered slowly, 'Well, she is pretty thin and tired, and she is even getting a few lines on her face. Her life is much too stressful.'

"Suzann sighed, 'I am so glad that we can have a much more serene and peaceful life here with the sons of God, where everyone loves and serves the Lord and people love and care for each other too.'

"The other thing Troy wanted to ask Jude about was if he thought there was a chance for him to buy back his old childhood home which his father had sold.

"'Yes, I think so. The owners are talking about moving up the mountain. However, I am afraid that they have allowed the house and garden to get a bit rundown,' Jude said. He agreed to go the next day with Troy to find out about it.

"They went to see the house the next day, and Troy bought it, in spite of all of its needs. He started right away in his spare time to remodel it with our help. He made a completely new front on the house. It had a porch, more windows, and a beautiful carved front door. After this he renewed the inside. When he had finished renewing the inside, he started on the garden. He cleared away all the weeds and trash and started planting beautiful shrubs, plants, and seeds from Grandma Eve's garden, which she was very happy to share. Melody was glad to help out too, as much as her time permitted. He planted some fruit trees at the back of the garden and dug a well, which turned out to be a flowing fountain in the middle of the garden. He surrounded it with a circle of bright flowers. There were stones around the flowers and four benches faced the fountain. Some evenings he and Melody would just sit there in the moonlight and talk.

"One afternoon Troy said to Melody, 'It is such a beautiful spring day of renewal, and we have both been working very hard. Could you possibly take a few hours off work so that we could take Beauty and Princess riding down by the river where we used to go? I'd like to see if there are any gold nuggets down there and if the buttercups and wild roses are still growing there.'

"'Yes, I would enjoy going there,' she said,

and then added, 'I'll pack a picnic lunch, and we can eat our supper by the river too.' The sun was warm, and the trees were leafing out with the delicate and soft lacy green of new growth.

"After arriving at the river, they took off their sandals and waded in, looking for gold nuggets, but they found only a few. Melody loved nature, especially the birds and animals. She had brought seeds and spread them on a big rock by the river for the birds. She would whistle at the finches, and they would answer her with their sweet songs. Troy enjoyed joining in with his flute.

"Troy sat across from Melody as they ate their lunch. The setting sun behind Melody cast a soft light through and around her long hair. It made a glowing halo of light around her pretty face. He just sat and looked at her and thought, *How beautiful she is! How could I not love her?* But he said nothing. When they had finished eating, he helped her put the lunch things away. Placing his arm lightly around her shoulder, he walked her over to Princess, and with a quick kiss on the top of her head, he helped her mount. As they rode home under the canopy of moonlight, not much was said, but as Melody told us later, she was thinking, *I do wonder if Troy will ever come to care for me in the same way that I love him!*" At the parting of the road, they said goodnight rather quickly, since Princess was waiting impatiently to gallop off toward home. It was happening slowly, but their love was unfolding like a rosebud, opening into a full blown and lovely rose in the warm spring sunshine.

"It was drawing near to the end of the week and to the seventh day. Troy waited by Melody's door at work until she could come out, and then he asked her, 'Melody, do you still go by the Garden of Eden to worship on the Sabbath day?'

"'Yes,' she answered, 'You know that the Lord made the seventh day holy at the end of the creation week when He rested from His work of creating the earth and everything in it. He has told us to keep the seventh day special, that we should rest from our work and remember His love for us. He knew that it was for our own good that we should have one quiet rest day every week. Things are a little different now than when you were here before. The men have built a simple chapel for our worship place in Grandmother Eve's garden. Sometimes an angel visits us to teach us important things; also, the elders instruct us.

"'I think that Enoch may be speaking to us this week. He is a very knowledgeable and righteous man. We do enjoy listening to him. Then we sing praises to God. It has been requested that I sing one of my songs this Sabbath. Would you like to come with us for Sabbath worship?' she asked.

"'I would love to come,' he answered. He had

just invented a new violin-like instrument, and he offered to play a soft background for her song if she would like for him to do so. They went over it together twice, and it sounded lovely. The harmony was perfect.

"Weeks later, after having taken Beauty out to the riverside pathway to run, Troy sat outside the building waiting for Melody to come out. When he saw her coming, he called to her, 'Melody, do you have a few minutes? I want to show you something.' She agreed, and they walked to his house and out behind to the garden, where he directed, 'You just sit on the bench, and I will bring it out.'

"He came back soon with a box that he set down beside her. The box was full of yellow baby chicks. She exclaimed, 'Oh, they are so sweet.' She picked one up to cuddle in her hands. 'I would like to take care of them for you.'

"Troy laughed and said, 'I was hoping you would say that! Dan gave them to me.' Dan loved animals and farming. 'He also gave me some chick feed to start off, and I built a little chicken coop behind the orchard. Hopefully, later on, we will have all the eggs we want and some to give away.'

"She liked the idea and decided to hurry right over to Dan's house to get instructions on raising poultry.

"The busy summer months went quickly by,

and autumn came with a burst of color.

"Suzann and Melody had been experimenting with combining different kinds of grains to see what would make the best tasting bread. They thought they had finally found the perfect combination, and Melody wanted to take a loaf to Troy to taste, but he wasn't at home. She went out into the garden and called him 'Troy, Troy, are you out here?'

"She heard a muffled reply, 'I'm here, up in the apple tree!' She took the bread into the house and hurried out to the back of the garden where Troy was picking apples. She held up the garden basket to make it easier for him to fill it. It didn't take long as the apples were very large. Once the basket was full, they sat down on a nearby bench and ate one between them, just to see if the apples were ripe enough to pick more. They decided that they were just right and that they would pick more the next day. Melody stood up, thinking that it was time to go home. She mentioned the fresh bread she had left in the house for him, and he thanked her. Then she paused for a moment to watch the sparkling, dancing fountain.

"The continual motion of the water with the sun shinning through it made an always changing and soothing picture, but to be honest, she just hated to leave and say goodbye to Troy. He stood up also, and looking at her earnestly, he asked her a question, 'Melody, do you like this garden?'

"'I surely do. I love this garden,' she answered, wondering why he asked that question.

"But then he asked another question, 'Melody, what do you think about this house?'

"'I have always thought you did a very good job of making it beautiful and livable,' she said.

"He paused a moment and then said quietly, 'I've really worked hard to make a success of the instrument manufacturing business.'

"'I know,' she interrupted.

"'But what you don't know,' he added, 'is that the business has now arrived at the place where we are doing very well, and I can finally tell you the desire of my heart. Melody, my dear friend,' he said holding out his hands toward her, 'I've always loved you very much. Would you, could you, consider being my wife?' and then he added hesitantly. 'You may take some time to decide if you need to.'

"But she didn't need time. She ran to him and melted into his arms. They silently clung to each other for a few minutes, and he gently kissed her apple sweet lips. Her heart swelled with the happy realization that she had finally found her home in his loving and protective arms. 'Troy,' she assured him, 'I don't need time to think about it! From the time we were little children, I've always depended on your care. You are the most important person in my life! I would love to be your forever friend and wife.'

"He drew her closer and kissed her again, smoothing her gleaming, long dark hair down her back, 'Melody, would it be all right with you if we bowed down here in the garden and asked our heavenly Father to bless our engagement?' Bowing by the garden bench, as each had an arm around the other, he prayed to his heavenly Father for His blessing on them and for help that they might always be faithful to Him and to each other through the years. She added her amen at the end of his prayer.

"Then they stood up, and he touched her soft cheek with his fingertips. 'My dearest,' he said, drawing her close to him again, 'today you have made me the happiest of men, and I will always try to be a good husband to you, and when we have children, I will work to be a good father to them also.'

"'I am certain that you will do just that!' she assured him. 'I love you very much, Troy,' she added as they sat down on the bench holding hands. 'You are really all that I want.' They briefly discussed some wedding plans, after which Melody asked, 'Would you like to go and tell my parents the good news of our engagement?'

"'Yes, let's go.' Carrying the basket of apples for Suzann, Troy walked Melody home, with stops along the way for just one more kiss!

"Her parents were delighted with the news, and Suzann said, 'Troy, do you remember that when you first came here I said that we would try to be parents to you? Now that you and Melody are getting married, that will be doubly so. We couldn't be happier about it, for we love you as a son already.'

"'That's true,' Jude added. 'I couldn't have had a better son than you are, Troy, for helping in the business and in every other way too, nor could we have found a better husband for our precious Melody. May God bless you two.' They both gave him a hug. Melody had been standing there happily smiling, and she quickly joined them for a four-way hug!

"The very next day Suzann went to find the shepherd with the best wool for sale. She, with the help of some of the other women, spun the finest of wool thread and wove a very soft and fine cloth for Melody's wedding gown. Suzann and her friends embroidered a ring of red roses around the neck of the dress and smaller ones around the hems of the wide sleeves. It was very beautiful.

"The whole community was deeply interested in the coming wedding, and they all wanted to be involved. Jude organized a small orchestra from his best music students, and they started to practice for the event. Molly's singing had improved a great deal with time, and she was anxious to sing for her favorite teacher's wedding. Troy and Melody asked the beloved, respected, and godly patriarch Enoch to conduct the wedding service. Dan and his wife were in charge of flower decorations, and Eve and a group of the women planned a special wedding feast.

"When the big day finally arrived, the whole community assembled in and around the little chapel near the Garden of Eden. The front of the chapel was banked with fragrant flowers. Jude and Suzann were a distinguished looking couple as they sat near the front of the chapel, and she was still a stunning lady in her new green gown. The orchestra played soft background music, and Molly sang her song before Melody appeared. When Melody came into view, everyone fell silent. She looked so radiant! Her soft wedding gown followed the lines of her lovely figure, and then it flared out to her ankles where her gold slippers just peeked out from the hem of her gown. Her only decoration was a red rose tucked into her long, dark hair and the roses she carried.

"Suzann had ordered some special new clothes tailored just for Troy, and he looked very handsome standing at the door waiting for Melody. It was a simple wedding. She took his arm, and they walked down the isle to where Enoch waited. They said their vows, and Enoch finished by saying, 'What God hath joined together, let no man put asunder.' Then he prayed and pronounced blessings upon them as they began their lives together.

"The orchestra played as they walked out to the garden to greet their friends and relatives. Nan and I helped serve the big wedding feast. So that is how Troy and Melody, our very dear niece and nephew, started their wedded life together."

Chapter 4

Sam pauses. The history of the early descendents of Adam and Eve fascinates you, and you wish for Sam to continue the story.

After a few moments of silence, he picks up where he left off. "Troy and Melody had a long and happy life together. Their first child was a daughter whom they named Lark. Lark, with her blond ringlets and big blue eyes, was Grandpa Jude and Grandma Suzann's little doll! When she was old enough, Troy occasionally took her riding on his horse to visit Grandpa Adam and Grandma Eve who loved her also. They were now beginning to show their age. However in all, Adam lived to be nine hundred thirty years old.

"Lark loved flowers and growing things. She found great joy in helping her father plant and harvest the garden, which he did in his spare time. She was very certain that her daddy couldn't get along without her help! After all, she could drop the beans into the holes that he made in the ground. He was very patient with her, and this gave Melody some time to get things done in the house. Lark couldn't wait until the time came when she could proudly march into the house carrying a big squash for her mother to cook! She was a very sweet little girl and was much loved.

"One beautiful, early summer morning after breakfast and morning prayers, Troy said to Melody, 'I still have a little time before I have to go to work, so I thought that I would run down to the pasture and check on Princess and Beauty and see how they are doing. Would you and Lark like to come along?'

"'Oh yes,' she answered. Then she said to Lark, 'Lark, horses just love apples. Shall we take some as a treat for them?' So they stuffed their pockets with apples and started down to the pasture. The horses were glad to see them, but they seemed more interested in checking on what was in their pockets!

"Lark was engrossed in feeding Princess with chunks of apples when Troy, pointing to a large shade tree some distance from them, exclaimed, 'Lark, look. Do you see something moving under that tree?' The figure moved and then turned around, and they could see that it was a little baby colt!

"He pranced and danced with the sheer joy of being alive, and then he raced as fast as his young legs could carry him back to his mother, Princess. Lark was so excited and happy that she jumped up and down. 'Oh Daddy, isn't he wonderful? Will he be mine? Can I ride him?'

"'Yes, he is yours, but you both have to grow a bit before you can ride him.'

"'I'm growing,' she said, stretching up as high as she could on her tip toes. Everyone laughed, and Melody explained that there were a lot of things that Lark could do first. The colt had to have a name, which she could pick out herself. Next, she must teach him that she is his friend. Then she must teach him to let her lead him. After that, Grandpa Jude had already promised that he would teach Lark how to ride and how to take care of a horse when she got one. It didn't take long for Lark to pick a name for her precious little colt.

"'Happy Horse is his name,' she announced, 'because he seems so happy to be able to run, and he makes me happy too!'

"So Happy it was from then on. Troy remarked

that he thought that Happy was going to take after his father, Beauty, as he loved to run.

"When Lark grew to be a young lady, she would take Happy to race on the riverside path with Beauty when Troy took him out for a run—every once in a while Happy would beat his father in a race.

"And so the years flew by with work and simple pleasures for this dear family. Two sons completed their family. Troy and Melody taught their children to love their heavenly Father and to care for each other. When the boys grew older, they helped to build Noah's ark with a group of other men, including Methuselah and his sons. (Methuselah lived to be nine hundred sixty-nine years old, the oldest man who ever lived.)

"The wood that they used for the ark was very hard. Actually you might think that it resembled stone. As you know, it took a very long time to build that huge boat. As he worked, Noah preached about the flood that God had said would come, urging the people to reform and change their sinful ways so that they could be saved. He preached for one hundred twenty years until the ark was finished. By the time it was finished, all of the sons of God had either joined Cain's group or had died. None of us, except Noah and his family, saw that strong and sturdy ark when it was finished, nor did we see that terrifying deluge that destroyed the then-known world.

"On the other hand, Cain's descendants had grown in number, and when the sons of God married the daughters of Cain, some of their sons were called men of renown because of their great inventions and intellect. However, because they had put God out of their lives and were worshiping idols of their own making, they became more evil and violent with every passing generation, taking what they wanted by force from their neighbors, even their neighbors' wives! They finally got to the place where they were always thinking about and plotting some sinful activity.

"It was at this point that God decided that He would wipe the earth clean by a flood, but He didn't send the flood without warning the people to change their ways and be saved. But the people did not heed the warnings. They scoffed and laughed at Noah and told him that what the Lord had told him to say about a flood was scientifically impossible.

"They said, 'How could a flood come now? The vegetation is watered by the dew and a mist.' They hardened their hearts and became more evil than before.

"After failing to heed the warnings, the people saw the miraculous sight of all kinds of animals marching two by two and by sevens into the ark, guided by unseen angel hands, and still they were unimpressed. After pleading with them one last time, Noah, his wife, and their three sons and their wives entered the ark. The angel closed the tremendously heavy door, which no person could open.

"When rain came pouring down from the sky and water came up from the ground, it was too late for those outside of the ark to be saved. Their imposing mansions and winding avenues lined by perfectly crafted statues and fruit trees that led to their idol altars on which they sometimes even offered their children were all swept away and destroyed by the raging flood waters. All people and animals were also swept away, and the earth was cleansed.

"As you know, the Garden of Eden has been restored to Adam and Eve here in the new earth. They are very grateful to God for giving them a second chance to live the peaceful and happy life they lived before they believed the serpent's lies and disobeyed God. They live near the river of life beyond here with their second son Abel. Their son Seth, who was born after Abel, is a very large and handsome man, who looks just like his father, Adam, resembling him more than his other sons do. He and his family live close to Adam and Eve also. A lot of their descendants, including Troy and Melody, have built their homes near the Garden of Eden. If you would like to meet

Hope for the Future

my relatives down there, I would be happy to take you there when you have time."

"I would be delighted! I feel as though I know them all already!"

"Then you add thoughtfully, "It is a real joy to talk to and to make friends with God's obedient children from every generation and every nation in the earth's history!"

By now you have climbed up to the last plateau, which is located very near to the top of the mountain. "Oh, I just love this place," you exclaim. "I could plant a garden and fruit trees here and make steps going up to the top where the house will be located." The view at the top is spectacular! You notice that in the new earth your senses—seeing, hearing, tasting, and smelling—are much enhanced.

As you gaze for miles across the landscape, you recognize the New Jerusalem, the holy city, resplendent and glowing in beauty. The sight nearly takes your breath away! God's glory emanates from that city—there is no night there because of His splendor. The city sparkles and shines as a beautiful jewel, even in the middle of the night. "I could never find a nicer place to build my country home, thanks to Jesus!" you say.

You have enjoyed your walk with Sam, but it is time to be getting back to Jerusalem. You hike down the mountain much faster than you climbed up it. You pause long enough to stop at the grape arbor to pick some grapes to take back to the city with you. Star is still by the waterfall. You put the grapes in your basket, and you and Sam ride back to the highway.

"The next time you come back, come over to my house. I will introduce you to Nan and the rest of my family, and I will take you to see our little neighborhood village, which I think you will find interesting."

You thank him and tell him how much you appreciate your day together, and that you are looking forward to meeting Nan and his family.

Chapter 5

Days later you return to the mountain, and as promised, you head directly to Sam's home. You find him working in his garden with a 10-year-old boy named Pravin who is busily helping him.

Sam introduces you to Pravin and then tells you a little about his story. Pravin's family was from India. They learned about God by listening to a Christian station on their little radio. They decided to worship the true God and not the elephant god and the other false gods in their home. They are so happy and grateful that they learned about God's free gift of salvation.

After Sam shares this information with you, Pravin pipes up, "I love visiting here with Sam and Nan. My parents said that I could stay for a week."

"I think they are special people also. What do you plan on doing for a whole week?" you ask.

"Oh, Nan already taught me to make some little pots for my mother, and I like to work with Sam. We will ride the horses and afterwards we will go down to the woods by the Riverside Park

Road, where he is going to make a swing on one of those tall trees for me. I have some friends here in the neighborhood whom I have fun playing with in the woods. We love to play with the animals. I really like it out here in the country," he says as he goes on picking berries.

Now Sam takes you over to Nan's pot manufacturing shelter at the edge of the garden. The shelter has a roof and three solid walls, but the front is made of lattice covered with vines bearing sweet smelling flowers of various colors with an opening in the middle. Sam takes you inside where you see Nan sitting at her wheel shaping a very large pot, which someone has ordered at her store in the village. Her friend Sue Lee is sitting at a table painting some very delicate and beautiful artwork on some other pots. Sam introduces you. You notice that Nan is tall, beautiful, and ambitious. She seems like a good mate for Sam. You thank her for her thoughtfulness in sending such a delicious lunch for you when you came to check out your new home.

"I was pleased to do it, and I'm glad you liked it. Please be patient with me," she adds. "I have only a few more turns to do on this pot and then it will be finished and ready to be placed in the kiln. After that I will be happy to show you around."

You walk over to where Sue Lee is sitting, and

Hope for the Future

you watch her painting for a few minutes, admiring her careful work. She is a sweet little Chinese lady, and as you compliment her on her work, she looks up and thanks you and says that she really loves doing the delicate decorations on the pots but that she also does landscape pictures. Nan explains that when Sue Lee arrived in heaven she had no relatives here, so they took her into their family, as no one should ever be lonesome in heaven. She fits in very well with them, and everyone is happy with the arrangement.

After a quick clean up, Sam and Nan are ready to take you to see their little village. Sue Lee wants to stay and finish the pot she has started painting, and Pravin decides to stay since Sue Lee is teaching him how to decorate pots, and he wants to finish the pots he is making for his mother.

You and Sam carry finished pots and one of Sue Lee's landscape paintings to put in Nan's store. He explains that the village is only a short walk beyond the bridge. It will be your village when you build your house on the mountain. Sam mentions that after arriving on the new earth, he has developed an interest in architecture, and he made the plans for the little village. Now you see a narrower gold paved road angling off to the left, which you follow to the end where you see the beautiful Lily Pad Village.

The village is square in shape and is surrounded by a low wall, and on the outside of the wall, you see lush green trees growing all around the village. It has beautiful double gates of wrought iron. Decorating the middle of each gate is a pink water lily on a small green lily pad made out of jewels that is surrounded by the graceful swirls and curls of the gates. The curls in the gate are interspersed with small goldfish that look as though they are swimming around the curves. Their gold sides glow with soft colors of the rainbow. On the arch above the gate you see written "Lily Pad Village."

"Does the work on that gate look familiar to you?" Sam asks.

"Well, yes it does. Could this be the work of Timothy, the man who decorated the bridge by my property?"

"You guessed correctly," Sam says. "Everyone

in the village voted to commission Timothy to create a gate that would reflect the heart of our village, namely the fish pond and its beautiful water lilies and pads."

Beyond the gate, the gold paving continues on everywhere—on the plaza and even on the floors of the stores. Each store has an open front with a pillar on each side of it and a high arch above it. There is a stately parade of royal palm trees, which are planted in front of each pillar, and bright flowers that surround the bases of the palm trees.

Anyone who owns property in the neighborhood may have a store there. However, he must pay a small tax for upkeep. Every month the treasurer of the village gives to each member a supply of their own coins for trading in Lily Pad Village only.

Across from the stores is a large pool with curbing around it. It is fed by an artesian well bubbling up at one end of the pool from a rock. The pool contains beautiful fish of all colors and descriptions. Delicate pink and white water lilies decorate the surface of the pool in calmer sections, from which the name of the village occurs.

Trimmed grass, potted flowers, and benches surround the pool, making it a nice place to stop, relax, and watch the fish.

You take the pots to Nan's store, and she

arranges them on the shelves while Sam hangs Sue Lee's painting on the wall with the others. You notice that some of the paintings look very familiar. There's one of the lambs playing on the slope of the river, another shows a beautifully colored blue bird sitting on a branch of a pink flowering bush.

You are happily surprised to see that the third painting is actually a depiction of the waterfall on your property with its delicate rainbow and lush surroundings. "I want to buy some of these paintings for my new house when it is finished," you tell Nan.

"Sue Lee is a very accomplished artist. She can paint anything you want any time that you want it."

Sam has his own store right next door to Nan's, but his space is more of an office than a store. You look in through the open archway from your location on the sidewalk. One of Sue Lee's paintings hangs behind a large desk with chairs in front of it. The rest of the walls are decorated with blueprints and maps, and he has all kinds of building materials displayed on shelves. He is good at helping people make decisions on how to build their new homes.

Sam points down the street toward a building that features a large all-purpose room and two classrooms. He informs you that you can register for a variety of classes at that building. In one an angel teaches astronomy. He starts by acquainting students with the nearby planets and galaxies where they can fly to on field trips later on.

Several people are waiting at Sam's office so he tells you to go on without him. "I really need to stop and help these people. I'll meet up with you and show you around more later."

With that, you take off on your own and check out some of the other stores. There's a bakery, a fresh fruit store, and a music store. You hear a great male quartet harmonizing in the music store, and you stop to listen. They are practicing at the back of the store. You step into the store and discover that Lucy is there with her baby Perry in a carrier on her back. She is looking at keyboards. You introduce yourself and tell her that you heard the men singing and thought that they were so good that you stopped to listen.

"Yes, they are very good, but their wives are good singers also, and they are now organizing a Lily Pad choir," Lucy says. "I want to thank you for being so nice to the twins when you came by."

"They are such good, well-behaved children. How could anyone help but love them!" you tell her. Then you ask her, "Where are Peter and Patty now?"

"The village always keeps a pot of fish food by the pool, and the children are allowed to feed them. If the fish happen to be hungry, sometimes they even jump out of the water to catch the food thrown to them," she says.

You look out toward the pool just in time to see Peter throwing a morsel out and a big yellow fish jumping out of the water to snatch it to Peter's great delight and Patty's squealing. "Quick, Peter, throw another one."

You ask Lucy if her baby is walking yet. "If you have a minute, I'll show you," she says while taking Perry out of the carrier. As soon as his chubby little feet hit the gold floor, he starts to make high-stepping motions. By this time the store owner, Joe, has finished with the quartet and is chuckling with you over Lucy's cute baby.

"I am going to start building my country home soon," you tell Lucy. "I want to have a neighborhood get-together when I finish. I'd like for you to come and bring your children."

"We would all love to come see your new place."

"Good. I'll be in touch. I'd best be going so that Joe can tell you all about his keyboards."

As you exit the store, you see a man sitting on a stool in front of the store. It is Barry, the wood carver who made the seats for the Little Bridge Park. You decide to visit his store and look at the exquisitely carved furniture and beautifully colored tapestries that he has on sale. You find a number of pieces that you would like for your new house once it is finished.

When you find the building where the astronomy class is being conducted, you step inside the door to quietly observe. One of the students looks familiar, and then you recognize that it is your friend Gene. He slips out to speak to you. "You just have to join this class," he says. "You know how much I have always enjoyed flying. Do you remember how I always wanted to take a space trip but never had the chance? Well, this class goes so far beyond that, that there is no comparison. The angel explains, as I understand it, the science of God's space creations—its vastness, its beauty, and its tremendous power.

"The angel also talks about the order of it all as each planet follows its assigned pathway around its sun and the planets' moons circle around it! But that isn't all, we are learning about the stars too. I personally am interested in learning more about galaxies and the black holes contained in them. Just think, God has names for each of these planets, and there are some that were created as perfect in every way as the Garden of Eden, and their inhabitants have never sinned as we did here on the first earth. What a privilege it will be to meet some of these wonderful people and to learn from their vast knowledge. We are very excited that we will soon be going on a field trip to visit some of the nearby stars we have learned about. Surely we never realized what a great God we serve and the greatness of His creations!"

You tell Gene that you are very interested in learning more about space also and that you will join the class as soon as you're able. You say a quick goodbye, and he goes back into the classroom. You thoughtfully start back toward Sam's office. On the way you stop to buy some bread and fruit. You then have a quick lunch at Sam's office, after which he brings out a large roll of house blueprints. You decide that you would like a stone exterior on your house with high pillars on the front, and you want a lot of big windows to give your house a bright and airy feeling that takes advantage of the great view.

Chapter 6

When your house is finished, you are delighted with it, and you invite your relatives and friends to build near you if they wish.

You are now ready to get more involved in Lily Pad Village activities. Sam has just been elected mayor of the village. He wants to see more classrooms built for educational purposes, and he would like to make some other additions to the village.

You have built a store in the village, but you haven't yet decided what to do with it. One beautiful morning after the gate has been opened and people are busy getting ready for the day, Mark appears and announces that Jesus is coming to visit Lily Pad Village the next day! Everyone is excited that Jesus will be visiting their little village, and they get busy cleaning and polishing their stores to make them look the very best for His visit.

When Jesus comes the next day with four of His attending angels, His face and garments glow with a great brightness and glory. As He holds out His hands toward you, you see flashes of light from the nail prints on His hands, which are the only reminders of His sacrifice for all humans. There is a look of tenderness, love, and care in His expression for everyone around him! Everyone bows in worship to the King of kings and Lord of lords.

Lucy then comes forward carrying baby Perry. Bowing again before Him, she requests that Jesus bless her baby. Jesus sits down on the bench beside the pool and takes Perry in His arms. He holds him close to His chest and pats him on the back as the baby cuddles and babbles baby talk. There is an instant bond between them! Then putting Perry on His knee, Jesus places one hand gently on the little boy's head and pronounces a blessing on him, after which He hands him back to Lucy. Lucy is delighted and thanks Jesus. Of course, other mothers want their babies blessed also. As Jesus blesses each one, everyone is reminded that we should be as sweet and trusting of our Lord as a child.

Hope for the Future

After blessing the little children and looking around the village, He tells you that He has come to take those who would like to go with Him on a walk to a small lake on the other side of the river where He will share with you some secrets of how things grow in nature, as every living thing has its own laws and order, and one thing depends upon another. After that He will answer your questions. Of course everyone wants to go! You walk over the bridge to the other side of the river.

It is a very pleasant hike through the lush green fields. When you arrive at the lake and are comfortably seated on some split log benches, Jesus explains to all those gathered about how every living thing works.

Two angels gather the children under a large tree and start teaching them a new song, after which they go to a sandy peninsula and make sailboats out of birch bark for the children to play with in the water. The children are having a wonderful time, and so are the adults, who are fascinated by the story of the creation of plants and animals and how they interact.

The other two angels hurry back to the city to get lunch for everyone. One of the special treats they bring back are delicately sweetened cakes made from manna. After lunch you thank Jesus for such a very special day. You also thank Him again for your beautiful mountain, which he prepared for you. You feel a closer bond with Him now that you've been in His presence, and you sense a deeper love and devotion to Him because of His great love and care for you. After this, you start back to Lily Pad Village, but first Jesus leads you to the tree of life, where you can pick all of the special fruit you want. Then one of the angels walks back with you to help you carry the fruit to your village.

It is now Friday, preparation day. People are busy cleaning their houses and themselves. When you arrived in heaven, Jesus gave you a beautiful white robe, a portable gold harp, and gleaming bright crown. As it is the day before Sabbath, you and everyone else check their robes to make sure there is no spot or wrinkle on them, and everyone polishes their crowns. You notice that some crowns are much more ornate than others, having intricate designs and decorations on them.

Hope for the Future

Perhaps the reason for this difference is that these people worked much harder to help others get ready for heaven. But everyone is happy and content with his or her crown.

On the next day, Sabbath, the neighborhood stirs early. Everyone wants to be ready when they hear Joe blow his trumpet on Riverside Park Road. Sam has made a standard, like the children of Israel carried when traveling. The standard helped to identify each tribe as they moved or went to war. Sam's standard is a long pole that stands when you set it down. At the top of the pole is a shield on which Sue Lee painted, on both sides, a pink water lily on its green pad. In a graceful curve over the top, is printed "Lily Pad Village."

At the appointed hour, Sam, carrying the standard, and Joe with his trumpet start at the village gate. After every sixty steps, they stop. Joe blows his trumpet, and the people from that neighborhood stream out and join the march behind Sam and Joe to the Holy City. Peter, Patty, and Pravin come running out and want to march with you. Pravin's family and Lucy are close behind you, and Nan is carrying Perry to give Lucy a rest. You boost Peter up on your shoulders and hold Patty's hand while Pravin walks close by. Your harp hangs by a strap over your shoulder. It's all great fun to the twins, but Pravin, being older and more thoughtful, asks about the standard. You explain that it is to identify the group and if he should get lost in the big crowd all he would have to do is look for the standard.

Gene sees you marching and rushes up to tell you something. "Our astronomy class has already visited some nearby worlds. They are not all barren and desolate as are the worlds and moon that scientists and astronomers studied on the old earth. Some are very beautiful and productive. Our next project will be to go and explore that great opening in the sky called Orion. Do you remember traveling through the colorful stars in Orion's belt when Jesus took us to heaven at the second coming?"

"How could I forget! What a spectacular display of brightly colored planets on both sides of that passage! Would it be possible for me to join your class at this late date? I have more time now."

Hope for the Future

"I'll find out," he promises as he hurries back to his group.

By this time Sam has collected most of the village members, and it is getting a bit noisy. He stops, puts down his standard, and starts playing a hymn on his harp. "We Are Marching to Zion" echoes over the crowd, and Joe begins singing in his rich baritone voice. His quartet joins in with him, and then you hear Lucy's sweet voice added to the singing. Soon most of the people are singing as they start marching along again.

> *We're marching to Zion,*
> *Beautiful, beautiful Zion.*
> *We're marching upward to Zion,*
> *The beautiful city of God."*

You are now within sight of the Holy City—Zion, the New Jerusalem as it is called. It is a very large square! The foundations of the high walls are of precious and colorful stones. The walls are of jasper and measure about 1,400 miles in length, and are as wide and high as it is long (Rev. 21:16). There are three gates on each side of the city, and each one is made of a single, shiny white pearl, which makes for a total of twelve gates all together. Angels are standing at every gate, and people are entering on all sides. You walk up the hill to the city with the rest of your friends and neighbors.

As you arrive at the gate, you see Mark helping the angel at the gate directing groups to their assigned places on the sea of glass. The sea of glass is a very large paved place where thousands of people can assemble. It has a clear, glasslike surface that allows you to look deep down below. The sea of glass reflects the flame of God's glory around you.

You are surrounded by a multitude of people who have come to worship God. They are all dressed in their gleaming white robes and are wearing their glittering gold crowns. King David and other dignitaries are there also, and they add their glory to the scene. That alone is an impressive sight, but that scene comes to nothing as your eyes sweep ahead of you to the great white throne of God where the seven lampstands are burning brightly, representing the Spirit of God, and the twenty-four elders, clad in their white robes and gold crowns, are sitting on their twenty-four thrones. His throne is imbued with such power and glory that occasionally lightning streaks forth from it, accompanied by thunder! On the throne you see your heavenly Father and His Son, Jesus, seated together. A beautiful rainbow arches over them, in appearance like an emerald, and thousands of thousands of holy angels attend them. You can hear their voices saying, "Holy, holy, holy!"

People in their first earthly bodies could have

never viewed this scene and lived. It is a solemn and sacred occasion. The brightness and glory of God is nearly overwhelming.

It is announced that the Father has now chosen the person to be honored this day by being invited to come up and sit with Jesus on His throne. "What a wonderful, inspiring, and happy experience that must be for the fortunate person who is chosen for that honor," you say to Sam. "Perhaps it will be one of His disciples."

"Remember, there is no limit to time here on the new earth. I think that everyone may have that honor at some time," Sam says.

Suddenly your name is announced. As you stand in amazement, two angels appear to escort you up the steps to the throne! You glance back at Sam who, with an encouraging smile, gives you a little push. The angels take your hands and easily help you climb up the many steep white marble steps to the top where Jesus is waiting on a very large gleaming white marble platform. He is surrounded by thousands of His attending angels, and many more are flying in and out, taking care of needs in the universe.

Jesus is there to welcome you and take you up the final steps to His wide, spacious, and intricately designed white throne. You are overwhelmed by His majesty. He takes your hand and says, "Peace be with you. You are being honored because we love you." A wonderful, happy, and peaceful feeling sweeps over you, and you sit down on His throne and look out over the whole expanse of that spectacular golden city with its transparent golden streets and beautiful mansions.

"Look over to the left corner of the city," Jesus says. "See, that is where your city home is located."

"Yes, yes, I can see it plainly," you say with pleasure.

The time has now come for the service to begin. Looking down you see the twenty-four elders arise from their thrones below, and facing the throne, they remove their crowns from their heads and cast them down before the Lord. Then they bow and lead the people in a prayer of praise, saying, "You are worthy, O Lord, to receive glory, and honor, and power, for You created all things and by Your will they exist and were created."

Next, the commanding angel who leads the music stands up on a low platform and, while tuning his harp, announces that he will play and sing "The Song of Moses and the Lamb," after which you will all join him in singing and playing it on your own harps. The ground literally vibrates with the sound of thousands of people skillfully playing and singing that beautiful old song that Moses composed so many years ago, after crossing the

Red Sea on dry land and watching their enemies be destroyed.

> *Great and marvelous are Your works,*
> *Lord God Almighty!*
> *Just and true are Your ways,*
> *O King of the saints!*
> *Who shall not fear You, O Lord,*
> *And glorify Your name?*
> *For You alone are holy.*
> *For all nations shall come*
> *And worship before You,*
> *For Your judgments have been*
>   *manifested"*
> *(Rev. 15:3, 4).*

Next, John the Beloved speaks. He talks about the love of God. He says, "'We love Him [God] because He first loved us' (1 John 4:19). 'Beloved, let us love one another, for love is of God … In this is love, not that we loved God, but that He loved us and sent His Son to be the propitiation for our sins. Beloved, if God so loved us, we also ought to love one another' (verse 7-11). Love is like a circular golden chain from God. Some of its links are self-denial, consideration, and devotion to other people's happiness. That is love. This is how God first loved us and gave His Son, Jesus, to suffer and die in our stead to save us from eternal death for our sins. Jesus loved us enough to come to earth and die in our place. Realizing this, our love and devotion are returned to the Father and Jesus. This love is extended to God's other dear people who have accepted His gift of eternal life and love Him. Thus they are included in this chain. So, you see, this golden circle of love renews itself and goes on forever with God's loving us and of our loving Him in return." Then John turns to the Father and says, "Thank you, Father and Jesus, for this great love. Thank you."

Next it is announced that King David will sing a new arrangement of the twenty-third Psalm, which was inspired by his experience as a shepherd boy. When he was a youth, he was called "the sweet singer of Israel." He wrote many songs for his temple choir and orchestra to sing and play, but his twenty-third Psalm is a favorite of many people. Now you see King David coming forward. His private orchestra files up onto the platform first. The musicians are followed by a tall, handsome, and regal-looking man who has wavy dark hair and a beard. His beautiful deep voice rings out,

> *The Lord is my shepherd;*
> *I shall not want.*
> *He made me to lie down in green*
>   *pastures;*

He led me beside the still waters.
He restored my soul;
He led me in the paths of righteousness
For His name's sake.
Yea, though I walked through the valley
    of the shadow of death,
I feared no evil; for You were with me;
Your rod and Your staff, they comforted me.
You prepared a table before me in the
    presence of my enemies;
You anointed my head with oil;
My cup ran over.
Surely goodness and mercy followed me
    all the days of my life;
And now I dwell in the house of the
    Lord forever!

Then David turns toward the throne and says, "Thank you, Lord, for being my Good Shepherd, and thank you that my friends and I are able to be here with you today." Then he and his whole orchestra bow low before the Lord before leaving the platform.

After this some of the sweetest and most intricate and harmonious heavenly music floats up to your ears from one of heavens choirs and orchestras. You were hoping that they would sing again, but it is time for Aaron to offer the benediction. Jesus explains to you that in the time of Moses and the children of Israel Aaron, Moses' brother, and his sons were appointed as priests. Jesus Himself told Aaron to repeat these words to Israel, and then they would be blessed. Now Aaron, a white-haired and bearded, solemn-looking man, stands on the platform, and in a clear and distinct voice he repeats again these words of blessing for everyone there,

> *The Lord bless you and keep you;*
> *The Lord make His face shine upon you,*
> *And be gracious to you;*
> *The Lord lift up His countenance upon you,*
> *And give you peace"* (Num. 6:24-26).

The heavenly orchestra plays and the choir of thousands of voices rings out with the amen chorus, which then slowly fades away to a softly whispered amen and amen.

The angels who escorted you to the throne have come to take you back to your group. You thank Jesus for giving you this wonderful experience. He places His arm around your shoulder and walks you down the staircase. Before you leave, He says, "You are one of my precious children. Go in peace."

Your heart is filled with a wonderful feeling of happiness, love, and peace as you descend the steps of the throne with your angel escorts.

Hope for the Future

And so the years fly by. You will always be youthful, healthy, and happy, developing in your chosen fields of learning with no end. Best of all, love pervades the heavenly courts. There are so many wonderful loving people and angels for you to meet and make friends with, and you are very much loved by your heavenly Father and Jesus, who was willing to give His life for you. You gratefully repeat these words aloud: "Thank you, Father; thank you, Jesus! Thank you! Amen and amen."

References

The following are some of the Bible verses I based this story on. God has given us glimpses into what the new earth will be like, but our minds can only begin to imagine what is in store for us in heaven.

> *But the day of the Lord will come as a thief in the night, in which the heavens will pass away with a great noise, and the elements will melt with fervent heat; both the earth and the works that are in it will be burned up.... looking for and hastening the coming of the day of God, because of which the heavens will be dissolved, being on fire, and the elements will melt with fervent heat? Nevertheless we, according to His promise, look for new heavens and a new earth in which righteousness dwells* (2 Peter 3:10–13).

Hope for the Future

I saw a new heaven and a new earth, for the first heaven and the first earth had passed away (Rev. 21:1).

The streets of the city shall be full of boys and girls playing in its streets (Zech. 8:5).

They shall build houses and inhabit them; they shall plant vineyards and eat their fruit (Isa. 65:21).

Joy and gladness will be found in it, thanksgiving and the voice of melody (Isa. 51:3).

But to you who fear My name the Sun of Righteousness shall arise with healing in His wings; And you shall go out and grow fat like stall-fed calves (Mal. 4:2).

Then I shall know just as I also am known (1 Cor. 13:12).

A pure river of water of life, clear as crystal, proceeding from the throne of God and of the Lamb (Rev. 22:1).

Blessed are those who do His commandments, that they may have the right to the tree of life (Rev. 22:14).

Unless you ... become as little children, you will by no means enter the kingdom of heaven (Matt. 18:3).

I will open your graves and cause you to come up from your graves (Ezek. 37:12).

From one Sabbath to another, all flesh shall come to worship before Me (Isa. 66:23).

And the street of the city was pure gold, like transparent glass (Rev. 21:21).

Hope for the Future

And the ransomed of the Lord shall return, and come to Zion with singing, with everlasting joy on their heads (Isa. 35:1).

I give them eternal life, and they shall never perish (John 10:28).

To him who overcomes I will grant to sit with Me on My throne, as I also overcame and sat down with My Father on His throne (Rev. 3:21).

To him who over overcomes I will give some of the hidden manna to eat. And I will give him a white stone, and on the stone a new name written which no one knows except him who receives it (Rev. 2:17).

And he that overcomes, and keeps My works until the end, to him I will give power over the nations ... as I also have received from My Father;

and I will give him the morning star [could that mean property in other worlds?] (Rev. 2:26–28).

We invite you to view the complete
selection of titles we publish at:

www.TEACHServices.com

Scan with your mobile
device to go directly
to our website.

Please write or email us your praises, reactions, or
thoughts about this or any other book we publish at:

TEACH Services, Inc.
P U B L I S H I N G
www.TEACHServices.com

P.O. Box 954
Ringgold, GA 30736

info@TEACHServices.com

Aspect Books titles may be purchased in bulk for
educational, business, fund-raising, or sales promotional use.
For information, please e-mail

BulkSales@TEACHServices.com

Finally, if you are interested in seeing
your own book in print, please contact us at

publishing@TEACHServices.com

We would be happy to review your manuscript for free.

www.ingramcontent.com/pod-product-compliance
Lightning Source LLC
Chambersburg PA
CBHW072031170426
43200CB00025B/2559